Stellar Quines and
The Royal Lyceum Theatre Edinburgh
present

Apphia Campbell
THROUGH THE MUD

First performed at The Royal Lyceum Theatre Edinburgh on 2 November 2023.

Cast

Assata Shakur	**Apphia Campbell**
Ambrosia Rollins	**Tinashe Warikandwa**

Creative Team

Original Music	**Apphia Campbell**
Director	**Caitlin Skinner**
Lighting Designer	**Emma Jones**
Musical Director	**Marie-Gabrielle Koumenda**
Sound Designer	**Joseph Degnan**
Video Designer	**Ellie Thompson**
Producer	**Wezi Mhura**
Production and Stage Manager	**Jessica Ward**
Deputy Stage Manager	**Katie Stephen**
Sound Engineer	**Tongwenyan Wu** (Parasol)

This edition was published alongside the revival at Summerhall during the 2024 Edinburgh Festival Fringe.

Cast

Assata Shakur	**Apphia Campbell**
Ambrosia Rollins	**Tinashe Warikandwa**

Creative Team

Original Music	**Apphia Campbell**
Director	**Caitlin Skinner**
Lighting Designer	**Emma Jones**
Musical Director	**Marie-Gabrielle Koumenda**
Sound Designer	**Joseph Degnan**
Video Designer	**Ellie Thompson**
Associate Video Design	**Heather Scott**
Producer	**Laura Clark**
Production Manager	**Suzie Normand**
Stage Manager	**Brad Hamilton**
Sound Engineer	**Tongwenyan Wu** (Parasol)

With special thanks to...

Jackie Crichton, Hannah Roberts, Callum Smith and everyone at the Lyceum. Creative Scotland, The Edinburgh Festival Fringe Society and Made In Scotland for their support of the show.

Thank you to Baltimore Resilience Project, It's About Time Archives, Roz Payne Archives, CIR Online, Nationaal Archief, Tim Harrison, The Immortality Music Records, Dan's Bits and Shaire Productions for use of the archival footage.

Through The Mud is a reimagined version of *Woke* by Apphia Campbell and Meredith Yarbrough which won a Scotsman Fringe First Award in 2017.

Content Warning

This show features depictions of racism, abuse, violence, has occurrences of strong language and racialised insults. The show deals with topics and themes that may be distressing or retraumatising to some audience members.

Cast

Apphia Campbell | Writer, Assata Shakur

Apphia, originally from the United States, graduated from Florida International University with a BFA in theatre performance. In 2013, her critically acclaimed piece, *Black Is The Color Of My Voice*, debuted in Shanghai to rave reviews. It sold out at the Edinburgh Festival Fringe in 2014 and has since toured the UK, selling out venues such as the St. James Theatre, Wilton's Music Hall, and Oxford Playhouse.

In 2017, her show *Woke*, co-created with Meredith Yarbrough, won a Scotsman Fringe First, a Highly Commended Award from Amnesty International, and was shortlisted for the Filipa Bragança Award and Scottish Art Club Theatre Award. In 2019, she made her West End debut with *Black Is The Color Of My Voice*. In 2022, *Black Is the Color Of My Voice* went on an extensive sold-out tour around the UK, starring Florence Odumuso with Apphia Campbell making her directing debut.

In 2023, she re-imagined *Woke*, for two performers as *Through the Mud*, which opened at The Lyceum Theatre in Edinburgh. In 2024, her play *Black Is The Color Of My Voice* opened in Australia, winning Best Overall Theatre and Physical Theatre at the Australian Adelaide Fringe Festival and going on to tour to Sydney and Melbourne where it continued to receive critical acclaim.

Tinashe Warikandwa | Ambrosia Rollins

Tinashe is a Scottish Zimbabwean actress. Theatre credits include Alix/Shona in Fin Anderson and Tania Azevedo's *A Mothers Song*, *Cinderella* at the King's Theatre, Glasgow and Doreen Hood in Dundee Rep's *The Steamie*. She also performed as a dancer in *The Princess Switch* on Netflix. Tinashe is a graduate from The MGA Academy of Performing Arts.

Creative Team

Caitlin Skinner | Director

Caitlin is Artistic Director and CEO of Stellar Quines. She is also one half of feminist theatre company Jordan & Skinner and director of new-writing theatre company Pearlfisher. She was formerly Artistic Director of the Village Pub Theatre and Associate Director at Pitlochry Festival Theatre.

Directing credits for Stellar Quines include: *Until It's Gone* by Alison Carr, *Sister Radio* by Sara Shaarawi, *Hope and Joy* by Ellie Stewart. Caitlin is also the co-host of *Quines Cast*, Scotland's feminist arts podcast.

Emma Jones | Lighting Designer

Emma is a lighting designer based in Scotland and works across theatre, dance, music and opera. Emma has worked extensively in Scotland and around the world. Previous credits include work with The Royal Lyceum Edinburgh, The Tron, Dundee Rep, The Citizens Theatre, Perth Theatre, The Byre, The National Theatre of Scotland, Scottish Opera, Royal Conservatoire Scotland, Derby Theatre, Polka Theatre, Charlotte Mclean and Collaborators, Curious Seed, shotput, Catherine Wheels Theatre Company, National Dance Company Wales, Danza Contemporanea de Cuba, Hiccup Theatre Company, Joan Cleville Dance, Solene Weinachter Dance, Scottish Dance Theatre. Previous credits with Stellar Quines include *The View from Castle Rock* and *Fibres*.

Marie-Gabrielle Koumenda | Musical Director

Marie-Gabrielle Koumenda is a French-Cameroonian musician, composer and singer-songwriter performing under the artist's name Djana Gabrielle. She has been honing her craft on the Scottish music scene since 2015, releasing music and performing at various concerts and festivals. Lately she has been combining her love for music and theatre and has worked with various companies including Lyra, Imaginate, National Theatre Scotland and Magnetic North. She is a first-time Musical Director on *Through the Mud*.

Ellie Thompson | Video Design

Ellie studied at the Royal Central School of Speech and Drama in London. After graduating she has worked in various video roles including video supervisor, video programmer, associate designer and video designer for productions.

As Video Designer, theatre includes: *Bluets* (Royal Court Theatre, London); *Black Sheep* (Curious Directive, Norwich); *Through the Mud* (Stellar Quines & Royal Lyceum Theatre, Edinburgh), *Lament for Sheku Bayoh* (Royal Lyceum Theatre, Edinburgh & National Theatre of Scotland & Edinburgh International Festival); *Her* (Strange Town Theatre, Edinburgh); *Den Kirschgarten / The Cherry Orchard* (Deutsches Schauspielhaus, Hamburg); *Christmas at Inverleith House* (Lightworks); *Meet Jan Black* (Gaiety Theatre, Ayr); *The White Bike* (The Space, London).

As Associate Video Designer, theatre includes: *Spindrift* (Curious Directive); *REALLY BIG AND REALLY LOUD* (Paines Plough); *The Journey* (Double M Arts & Events); *Nuclear Future* (Gameshow); *Orlando* (Schaubühne, Berlin); *La Maladie de la Mort / The Malady of Death* (Théâtre des Bouffes du Nord, Paris); *Schatten, (Eurydike sagt) / Shadow (Eurydice Speaks)* (Schaubühne, Berlin).

As Video Designer, opera includes: *BEAM, Everybody can stand in their own light* (Britten Pears Arts); *Judith: Konzert Für Orchester / Herzog Blaubarts Burg - Judith: Concerto for Orchestra / Bluebeard's Castle* (Bayerische Staatsoper, Munich).

Stellar Quines

Stellar Quines are an intersectional feminist theatre company for Scotland, dedicated to exploring the role theatre has to play in creating gender justice for all. Our work is fuelled by artists, audiences and communities who want to see a better future for women, non-binary people and people of other marginalised genders. We work to create opportunities for them to flourish through theatre productions, Young Quines youth drama groups, engagement programmes and practitioner development.

stellarquines.co.uk

The Royal Lyceum Theatre Edinburgh sits at the heart of the city in our 140-year-old building welcoming over 100,000 people each year.

At the Lyceum, we believe that theatre is good for the soul. Led by our Artistic Director David Greig, we bring the best theatre from around the world to Edinburgh and share the best of Scottish theatre with the world.

We're experts in making theatre. We rehearse in our studio space across the road from the auditorium, and our costumes and sets are designed and built in house at our workshop in Roseburn, Edinburgh.

Community is at the heart of what we do. In 2024, our creative learning department celebrates 25 years of developing and nurturing talent. Our Youth Theatre programmes have been the starting point for many Scottish actors, fostering newfound confidence and lifelong friendships. We also host 60+ writing groups, technical courses and training.

Over the past 59 years the Lyceum has continued to make world-class theatre – take a seat, and experience it for yourself.

lyceum.org.uk

THROUGH THE MUD

Apphia Campbell

Characters

ASSATA, *mid to late thirties, strong and grounded in her beliefs*
AMBROSIA, *eighteen, naive, young, innocent*

All other characters are played by the two performers:
TREY, *twenties, a college student, knowledgable, confident*
PARAMEDIC, *any age, any race, a concerned professional*
JUDGE, *arrogant, white*
NJ POLICE OFFICER, *white, any age*
COLLEGE STUDENT, *early to mid-twenties*
PROFESSOR, *Black, energetic, passionate*
BPP MEMBER, *female, young, determined*
SANDRA, *thirties, Asatta's friend, grounded*
EVELYN, *thirty-five, a lawyer*
GRANDMOTHER, *sixties, worldly*

Notes on Text

A forward slash (/) denotes overlapping dialogue.

This text went to press before the end of rehearsals and so may differ slightly from the play as performed.

Scene 1

An opening soundscape: the political climate in Ferguson, Missouri, protest sounds, chanting, the sound of the crowd, etc.

We then hear about ASSATA SHAKUR *being wanted for murder, and the government is out for her arrest.*

All this merges into a slow guitar playing of 'St. Louis Blues' by W. C. Handy.

AMBROSIA *sings the first verse and the chorus.*

Scene 1.5

Ambrosia's world. Ambrosia's childhood home.

AMBROSIA. I remember the first time I heard that song, 'St. Louis Blues'. Bessie Smith, she recorded it in 1925 but it was originally recorded by W. C. Handy.

Bet you didn't know that. It was first time any blues was played in a minor key. Bet you didn't know that either. Something about that melody made me wonder what kind of women lived in St. Louis. People always said, 'That song's about sadness.' But you know what I heard?

AMBROSIA *sings a line from Bessie Smith's version of 'St. Louis Blues'.*

I always thought it was a song about adventure, and that glamorous women lived in St. Louis. And I'm gonna be one of them. I don't know why. I know it's not that same as it was back then.

But there are some things about a city that never changes. The sound. Growing. Evolving. But the soul, the root, it remains.

About a week before I left Pittsburgh to move to St. Louis, the shooting of Mike Brown happened. Things are heating up in Ferguson. After the incident, people are angry. Some want revenge.

A white cop shoots a seventeen-year-old Black boy and leaves his body lying in the street for four hours. They won't even let his mama through the police tape to see his body. People want answers. The top has come off that shaken soda bottle and no one can stop the explosion. Dad thinks I'm putting myself in danger, 'Don't you get caught up in that mess,' he said. We are a family who loves and supports the police. All lives matter and when people disobey the law, they need to be punished. They say Mike Brown was robbing a store when he was shot. Or he was escaping a robbery. It's all so scary to think about. Not exactly what I was expecting for my first semester at college. But I am going to be freeeee. Truly free. Make my own choices, come and go as I please. Dad cut me off 'cause he wants me to be a dentist like him, but I decided to study voice instead. I got a scholarship to Washington University and I am determined to prove Daddy wrong. In the end he can't say no to me, so he packed me and my things and drove me all the way from Pittsburgh to Missouri. Talked the whole time. 'Once you hold an electric tooth scaler and see the power in your hands, I'm sure you'll change your mind. You have to take over the business. I worked too hard to give it to somebody else.'

As we finished unloading, I quote Langston Hughes: 'I don't have to do nothing but eat, drink, sleep, sing, stay Black and die.' He rolled up the window and drove off.

AMBROSIA *sings*.

I guess I'm really on my own.

Scene 2

Ambrosia's world. Present day. University classroom. A school bell is heard.

PROFESSOR. Good morning, everyone. Welcome to African American Literature; the birthplace of the revolution. This year, 2014, marks one hundred and forty-nine years since Blacks were freed from slavery. It's not that long. I thought given the times we're in, I'd change the syllabus a little bit and begin with a woman who just last year was put on America's most wanted terrorist list. In 1977 she was convicted of killing a New Jersey police officer and sentenced to life in prison. She escaped prison and fled to Cuba, where she continues to live to this day. Ladies and gentlemen, Assata Shakur, the most wanted woman in America.

Scene 3

Assata's world. New Jersey Turnpike. Three gunshots are heard.

Lights shift to show ASSATA*'s entrance – her standing in the spotlight.*

AMBROSIA *becomes a* NJ POLICE OFFICER, *her hands raised as if holding a gun. She stands in the shadows with only her hands visible pointed towards* ASSATA*'s head.*

ASSATA. Mouth dirty.
   Grit.
   Arm numb.
   Body aching.
   I hear them asking –

NJ POLICE OFFICER. Is she dead yet? Ain't she dead yet?

ASSATA. My body lifts in the air. Onto a stretcher.

'America the Beautiful' by Katharine Lee Bates begins playing in the background.

Chest heavy.
Paramedics look concerned.

PARAMEDIC. Where's she hit? Where's she hit?

ASSATA. But the ambulance waits.
Pain.
So much pain.
I leave my body and go to another place.
Singing.
Music.

(*She sings.*) America, America,
God shed his grace on thee
And crown thy good with brotherhood
From sea to shining sea

AMBROSIA (*joining the singing*). America, America,
God shed his grace on thee
And crown thy good with brotherhood
From sea to shining sea

ASSATA. When I was young.
I use to read a lot.
And my mind was filled
Filled with these images.

AMBROSIA *dons the American flag and slowly begins waving it.*

I would read these books.
About adventures
That made me imagine that the world was such a beautiful place.
And if
And if the South
You know,
Could just be like the North

Then everything would be alright.
I would dream like

ASSATA *and* AMBROSIA (*singing*). America, America.
God shed his grace on thee

ASSATA. Even when I was dog thirsty
And couldn't drink a drop of piss-yellow water from the fountain.

AMBROSIA (*continues singing*). And crown thy good with brotherhood
From sea to shining sea.

ASSATA. Even when they burned crosses
At Ms Jenkins' house
Down the street.

(*Sings*.) America, America. God shed his grace on thee

As ASSATA *sings,* AMBROSIA *removes the flag from around her shoulders and drops it to the floor.*

And crown thy good with brotherhood
From sea to shining sea.

A school bell rings.

Scene 4

Ambrosia's world. Present day. Washington University.
AMBROSIA*'s first day of college.*

AMBROSIA. First day of African American lit class, and we're already in a heated debate about the Black Panther movement from the '60s and how it compares to the Black Lives Matter movement going on today. This guy in my class who acts like he's the professor says:

TREY. Even with the progress made in the '60s, that doesn't change the fact that Black folks are still treated like a colonized people.

And these riots are just a reaction – a consequence to the violence we face everyday. But the media wanna call us thugs and hoodlums.

AMBROSIA. I don't think I've ever heard the media use those words.

AMBROSIA *pauses*.

One girl calls me an Oreo. An Oreo?! Black on the outside, white in the middle.

Beat.

(*To* TREY, *arguing*.) What does 'Black Lives Matter' mean anyway? Times in the '60s were different. We had segregation, Jim Crow laws, denial of basic human rights. You mean to tell me that you think that everybody in prison has some sort of conspiracy against them? The system is scheming to put all two million of them in jail? All of them?

TREY. Well, if that's not the case then tell me why in Ferguson alone, 93% of arrests every year are African Americans? And why there are 33,000 warrants for only 21,000 people?

AMBROSIA (*to the audience*). I don't know what to say to that – I don't have facts.

(*To* TREY.) 33,000 warrants for only 21,000 people?

TREY. Pretty crazy, huh? If you wanna see what's really going on, why don't you take a day trip on over to Ferguson, pretty girl?

AMBROSIA (*to audience*). Then he smiles. Not a mean smile. A cute one. Dimples piercing through his scruffy beard. And in that moment, I couldn't decide if I should hit him or –

(*To* TREY.) Maybe I will. Check it out.

TREY. Cool.

AMBROSIA *moves to leave*.

AMBROSIA. Hey, what's your name?

Drums from 'Who Better Than You' begin.

Scene 5

Assata's world. Assata's hospital room. The drums continue.

ASSATA. They trying to break me.
Hateful words.
Arm paralyzed and bandaged.
Legs cuffed to the hospital bed.

NJ POLICE OFFICER. What's your name?

ASSATA. They keep askin' my name.

NJ POLICE OFFICER. What's. Your. Name.

ASSATA. They'll kill me if they know who I am.

I tell the Black nurse my slave name: Joanne. Joanne Chesimard.

She calls my family.

NJ POLICE OFFICER. Jiggaboo.

ASSATA. Cops beating me where bruises won't show.

NJ POLICE OFFICER. Nigger. Nigger.

ASSATA. With every hateful word, I keep my grandmother's voice chanting in my head:

(*She sings.*) Who better than you?
No nobody.

NJ POLICE OFFICER. DARKIE.

ASSATA. No nobody. Keep that head up.

NJ POLICE OFFICER. Speak up, girl.

ASSATA. Yes, who?

NJ POLICE OFFICER. Speak up!

ASSATA. Yes, yes, yes, Grandmother.

NJ POLICE OFFICER. COON.

The music stops.

ASSATA (*to herself*). I was born Joanne Deborah Byron.

NJ POLICE OFFICER. We know who you are now, Joanne.

ASSATA (*to herself*). I lived with my mother, my grandpa, and Grandma Lulu in Wilmington, North Carolina.

NJ POLICE OFFICER. Your honor, the defendant is ready.

The music resumes.

ASSATA (*to the judge*). This is a hospital room – not a court. Where's my lawyer? I want my lawyer!

NJ POLICE OFFICER. Now she speaks.

ASSATA (*to the audience*). My grandma always said: Keep your head up, Joanne, you're as good as anybody else.

JUDGE. All rise.

ASSATA (*to the audience*). And don't let nobody take advantage of my grandbaby.

(*To the* JUDGE.) I want my lawyer present.

JUDGE. You are charged with illegally resisting a lawful arrest and discharging a dangerous pistol.

ASSATA (*to* JUDGE). In the spirit of those unjustly and illegally charged before me:

JUDGE. You are charged with unlawfully and illegally assaulting officer James Harper / with intent to kill.

ASSATA. Fred Hampton. Angela Davis. / Lil Bobby Hutton.

JUDGE. You are charged with illegal possession / of a weapon.

ASSATA. I am a revolutionary.

JUDGE. A .38 caliber / automatic pistol.

ASSATA. I am a warrior –

JUDGE. Committing the crime of murder.

ASSATA. I am – [*innocent*]

The music stops abruptly.

Single spotlight on ASSATA *standing center stage.*

I entered Manhattan Community College in 1965 at the height of the Neo Negro revolution. All around me were Black and Third World students tuned in to what was happening in the world. I wanted to find my purpose. I wanted to know who I was – what I was meant to do.

African drums start.

COLLEGE STUDENT (*singing*). Hey, yeah, yeah, yeah.

ASSATA. Everybody was fighting for something.

COLLEGE STUDENT (*protesting*). Ain't none of these oppressors gonna give our children the education they need to overthrow them. That's why we need a say in the curriculum – so we can help our children become free.

ASSATA. Hey, yeah, yeah, yeah...

COLLEGE STUDENT.... Anything that has any kind of value is made, mined, and produced by working people. So why shouldn't working people collectively own that wealth?

ASSATA (*she sings*). Hey, yeah, yeah, yeah.

COLLEGE STUDENT. The police occupy our community, like foreign troops occupy territory.

ASSATA. Hey, yeah, yeah, yeah. First, we take control of the hospitals. Colleges – We'll have community controlled employment for city, state and federal agencies.

(*She sings:*) Hey, yeah, yeah, yeah yeah
Hey, yeah, yeah, yeah,
Hey, yeah, yeah, yeah,

They called me Sister.
African Queen.
A Goddess.
And she I became:
A beautiful, Black, loud-talkin', defiant-as-hell African, right there in New York City.
Wooo!

ASSATA *sings 'Jin-Go-Lo-Ba' by Babatunde Olatunji.*

COLLEGE STUDENT *joins in.*

ASSATA *and* AMBROSIA. JOANNE, JOANNE, JOANNE

Music volume lowers.

ASSATA. Joanne?! Joanne?! That won't do. I mean, Joanne is so… white.
Chesimard.
Foreign.
European.
The name of the Massa.
How many slaves did he own in Martinique?
Work to death?
Beat to death?
I need a new name.
A beautiful African name.
Like Kenyatta.
Or Nandi.
Or Assata.
Yes, Assata. She who struggles.
That's me.
I divorced my old life. And met my new husband.
The Black Panther.

ASSATA *and* COLLEGE STUDENT *sing.*

AMBROSIA *and* ASSATA *continue to dance as the lights shift back to Ambrosia's world.*

Scene 6

Ambrosia's world. Present day. A rally in Ferguson.

AMBROSIA *comes out of the dance still bubbling with excitement. She approaches the microphone.*

She stands, counting under her breath.

AMBROSIA. Hi. Rest in peace, Mike Brown.

She sings the first verse of Bessie Smith's 'A Good Man is Hard to Find'.

She strikes a pose.

Everybody's staring at me like I stood up here naked. In hindsight, it might not have been the best idea to sing Bessie Smith's 'A Good Man is Hard to Find' at a memorial for Mike Brown. The city has been exploding. Literally exploding. Tear gas. Curfews. Lootings. Burnings. Ferguson is on fire. Mom and Dad have been calling every day tellin' me to stay away from it all. But I've been reading Assata's biography, and she said:

ASSATA. 'It's our duty to fight for our freedom. It is our duty to win. We must love each other and support each other. We have nothing to lose but our chains.'

AMBROSIA. I started thinking: do I have chains? Am I bound? Shouldn't I just go over to Ferguson and have a look? And that's when I heard they were looking for talent to sing at Mike Brown's rally. I figured, I'd come, sing my song, break the chains.

Beat.

The air in St. Louis, is so thick with anger you can hardly cut through. That guy from class, Trey, comes up to me:

TREY. Find any good men with that song?

TREY *laughs*.

AMBROSIA. He thinks he's sooo funny. But when he gets on stage I'm mesmerized by the strength of his voice.

TREY. How many times must we turn from one cheek to the other and back again before our flesh is raw and our nerves are screaming? We've watched – for years – as police forces have moved into our neighborhoods like troops in a foreign land. They speak of welfare and protection, but all we continue to see is their oppressive harassment, their brutality, and we feel the pain from the murdered bodies left lying in the streets. Now we all know that with every turn of the wheel brings progress. Brings change. And right now, we got the power to push that wheel, to guide it. 'Cause this is our home. And we not gon' let cynicism be the mud that gums up our wheel. We've sat on the sidelines for too long, with less than 15% of Ferguson voting in the city council election. The city council appoints the chief of police. That's why next election, we gon' show up in force. Am I right?

The crowd cheers.

But in the meantime, in this darkness before the dawn, we got a light.

TREY *pulls out his iPhone and clicks on the flashlight.*

Shining. Recording.

The lights go down on TREY. AMBROSIA *continues to look on in the direction where he was, frozen in thought.*

The sound of multiple voices chanting: 'No more pigs in our community.'

Scene 7

Assata's world. Black Panther Party (BPP) offices. An archival video plays with the BPP singing. When ASSATA *speaks, a* BPP MEMBER *continues to hum the song.*

ASSATA *and* BPP MEMBER *fold newsletters.*

ASSATA/AMBROSIA. No more brothers in jail
   Off the pigs the pigs are gonna catch hell
   Off the pigs no more brothers in jail
   Off the pigs.

   The pigs are gonna catch hell
   Off the pigs no more pigs in our community.
   Off the pigs.

No more pigs in our community.
Off the pigs.

ASSATA. A few months ago, I officially joined the Black Panther Party.

(*Shouting.*) OFF THE PIGS!

I'm so ready I'm so –

A phone rings.

BPP MEMBER. Hello, Black Panther Party. Hello? Hello?

ASSATA. I got all these ideas in my head.
All this anger Like a fire.
In my gut.
Right here.
I gotta use it for good
Or I'm gonna explode.
I'm tellin' you.

A phone rings.

BPP MEMBER. Hello, Black Panther Party. Hello? Hello?

ASSATA (*singing*). No more pigs in our community.

BPP MEMBER. Off the pigs.

ASSATA. Right on, Sister.
These cats are amazing.
I never seen anything like this.
Sure, there some problems, internally.
They can get kind of radical.
Especially this cat named, Kamau.
He walks around quoting Fred Hampton: I believe I'm gonna die high off the people… a revolutionary in the international revolutionary proletarian struggle.

A phone rings.

BPP MEMBER. Hello, Black Panther Party. Hello? Hello?!

ASSATA. I dig it. I dig it.

We're taking it to the streets, policing the police, carrying guns.

Legally.
The ofays hate that.
But what we're doing is helping people.
We wanna uplift our community.
Somebody's gotta give us some freedom even if it means by force.

The sound of helicopters overhead.

ASSATA. They circling round here like flies that smell rot.

(*Yelling.*)
We aren't doing anything wrong.
Oh, how dare us, we give away free breakfasts to Black babies. We organize student rallies.
Give out free newspapers.
We patrol our own streets. And get this, we even gon' start our own clinics.
Black doctors for Black people.
NO MORE PIGS IN OUR COMMUNITY.
OFF THE PIGS.
NO MORE PIGS IN OUR COMMUNITY.
OFF THE PIGS.

Scene 8

Ambrosia's world and Assata's overlap. AMBROSIA *is at the Ferguson Rally,* ASSATA *is at the BPP offices.*

ASSATA *continues to sing the song while* AMBROSIA *joins in the present-day chant.*

AMBROSIA (*chanting*). NO JUSTICE.
NO PEACE.
NO JUSTICE.
NO PEACE.

We've been at this rally all day.

ASSATA. I joined the Black Panther Party because I wanted to make a difference.

AMBROSIA. It's starting to get dark, the police just arrived.

ASSATA. I wanted things to change, I believed they would.

AMBROSIA. The police start roundin' everybody up, telling people to go home.

ASSATA. We'd protest peacefully, walking with our arms linked together.

AMBROSIA. Someone says into the megaphone:

Peaceful protest is not disorderly conduct.
It's our First Amendment right to be here.

ASSATA. Peaceful protest is not disorderly conduct.
It's our First Amendment right to be here.

AMBROSIA. No one needs to go home.

ASSATA. The cops would respond with water hoses, loud-ass barking dogs biting people, leaving bodies lying battered in the streets.

AMBROSIA. No one knows what to do next. It's a standoff – like the ones you see in those Western films. Police on one side. Protestors on the other.

AMBROSIA. Police bang batons on the cars.

TREY. Police bang batons on the cars.

AMBROSIA. They start checking IDs left and right. Trey says they're checking to see who has a warrant for their arrest? Trey says:

TREY. Most people in Ferguson are scared of getting IDed. The police issue bogus tickets. Like $150 for illegal parking. Or $100 for jaywalking. People round here can't afford that.

So, when they get a ticket?
They gotta go to court.
They can't get to court? They go to jail.
They can't pay their ticket? They go to jail.
The judge writes warrants all day long.

'Cause that money is what keeps the whole police department running. I've got unpaid tickets in three different municipalities in St. Louis?!

AMBROSIA. Trey, are you insane?! Are you trying to get arrested today? Let's go. *But he just grabs the megaphone again:*

TREY *and* AMBROSIA. The police can't arrest someone

AMBROSIA. For being in a place.

TREY. There has to be illegal activity to arrest someone, otherwise it violates our Fourth Amendment rights which are protection from illegal search and seizure.

AMBROSIA. I don't know whether it's Trey with his megaphone, or the police in their SWAT gear, but the energy shifts. I feel it. Like when you feel a spider web on your skin but can't see it. I go stand on the sidewalk, out of the crowd. And I'm standing there under a tree when this cop comes up to me, asks to see my ID, then hands me a ticket, and says I better go before he writes me another one.

(*To cop.*) Illegal manner of walking in roadway? What does that even mean? I'm on the sidewalk – I don't need to 'disperse', it's my First Amendment right to be here. The cop gets that wide-eyed, raised-eyebrow look like he can't believe I dare talk back to him. Prints another ticket out of his gadget thingy for 'failure to comply.'

She looks closely at the ticket.

Wait, is this number the fine? $175 for failure to comply?

Shuffles the first ticket to the top.

$156 for illegal manner of walking in roadway?

I can still hear Trey through his megaphone. Talking about how the Fourteenth Amendment guarantees equal protection under the law. But suddenly he stops short, they tackle him like a quarterback holding the ball. He starts yelling: Illegal seizure! Illegal seizure!

I can hear the scuffle through his megaphone. Trey? Trey! Trey!!! Did anyone see the guy with the megaphone? The guy with the megaphone, did you see where he is?... Oh my god, is he breathing? Where are you taking him? He's hurt, can't you see that? I turn around and there's that cop again with a third ticket: 'Failure to disperse.'

Scene 9

Assata's world. Assata's home. ASSATA *is pacing up the Black Panther offices.*

BOBBY SEALE (*voice-over*). Information was received via the Black Panther Party National Headquarters this morning, that some ten or twelve members of the Black Panther Party in New York have already been arrested and others are being arrested, all by surprise. With pigs having drawn guns, and busted down Panther members' doors while they are sleeping...

An old rotary phone rings.

ASSATA *stares at it, then picks up on the third ring.*

ASSATA. Hello, Black Panther Party. Hello? Who the hell is this? Stop calling me. I haven't done anything. It wasn't me.

ASSATA *and* AMBROSIA (*singing*). Young blood
They killed you yesterday
But I saw you walking round today

Young blood whose got no time to waste
In strange lands where freedom waits

Black skin
Sweaty skin
Shining
Muscles bulging tight
They thought they killed you yesterday

Young blood
But they can't stop your fate.

As the track takes over, we see ASSATA *prepping to go underground as* AMBROSIA *lives her normal life, doing yoga, etc.*

A video shows news clippings of Ferguson vigils, and Black Panther Party sit-ins.

ASSATA *and* AMBROSIA *continue to sing.*

Scene 10

Ambrosia's world. Ambrosia's dorm room.

AMBROSIA. Hi, can you transfer me to the court clerk, please? Thank you!

She waits.

Hi, I'm calling because I got a ticket, well quite a few tickets at the Michael Brown rally last week, well, it wasn't really a rally, it was more of a gathering to, you know, talk about Michael Brown. I'm sure the judge will dismiss my tickets when he hears my side of the story. I mean, I know there's been looting. But I had nothing to do with that. I was just standing there, I… oh hello? Yes, I'm sorry have I been on hold? Yes – oh, Ambrosia Rollins, August 9, 1995, yes from last week.

Beat.

Oh okay, well I have class that day is there any way the judge can see me a bit later – ? Oh okay. No, I'll be there on time. Thank you.

Scene 11

Assata's world. Sandra's house. ASSATA *shows up to her friends house wearing glasses, a scarf around her head, and a muted sweater. She knocks.*

SANDRA *opens the door.*

SANDRA. It's too late for me, go save somebody else.

ASSATA. Sandra, it's me. Assata.

SANDRA. Joanne? Girl, get yo ass in here.

ASSATA. My picture is –

SANDRA. I know. You okay?

ASSATA. I'm surviving.

SANDRA. Where you going?

ASSATA. Imma hook up with some people I know.

SANDRA. Where you haveta meet 'em?

ASSATA. Ion know yet.

SANDRA. You got any money?

ASSATA. A few dollars.

SANDRA. Where you gon' go?

ASSATA. I'm figuring it out –

SANDRA. Girl, you militants ain't got no kind of sense, and will you take that shit off your head – you look like you 'bout to go bobbing for apples or some shit.

Beat.

You tell anybody you was coming here?

ASSATA. Nobody even knows we know each other.

SANDRA. Good. Good. They rounding y'all up like eggs on Easter Sunday. I walked by the Black Panther offices earlier, it's all boarded up.

ASSATA. The leaders have started shutting down the free programs. I saw Kamau and some of the other Panthers carrying machine guns.

SANDRA. It's war now.

ASSATA. First they say I killed two police officers. Now, I shot and killed some drug dealer?!

SANDRA. But you didn't, right?

ASSATA *looks at* SANDRA.

ASSATA. Why would I kill a drug dealer?!

SANDRA. Why they trying to jam you up so hard, sis?

ASSATA. I don't know. I don't…what am I gon' do?

SANDRA. We gon' figure it out.

ASSATA. All I wanted was to do a lil bit of good in my lifetime. Lay down a new foundation. But now, Imma criminal?

SANDRA. Don't fix your mouth to say that.

ASSATA. And that woman in the bank robbery picture – who in they right mind would think that's me?! She don't look nothing like me.

SANDRA. It was in the paper again today.

ASSATA. Shit.

Beat.

Maybe I should just go in, they'll see it ain't me.

SANDRA. Are you crazy?! I just read that the FBI can make it look like you were somewhere you ain't been. They take your picture and put it in a room, bank, shit, anywhere they want.

ASSATA. For real?

SANDRA. For real.

ASSATA. I shoulda never came here.

SANDRA. Girl, stop.

ASSATA. Got you involved in my thing –

SANDRA. Woman, will you please just shut-up? If I didn't wanna be involved I wouldn't have opened that door. I'm your friend. And I'm here for you.

ASSATA. Thank you.

SANDRA. Now will you go wash off that Underground Railroad smell you got going on. Girl, you funky.

ASSATA smiles.

Good to see you smile.

Beat.

After you wash up, come help me peel some potatoes for dinner.

ASSATA. I can do that.

SANDRA. Take whatever you need from the closet. This your home for as long as you need it.

ASSATA. Thank you.

SANDRA *leaves.*

The sound of three gunshots.

The lights go black on the stage, and ASSATA *stands center with only her face and shoulders lit.*

A voiceover is heard of ASSATA *describing being captured. As* ASSATA *walks to the courthouse the piano from 'Young Blood' plays.*

ASSATA *makes her journey to the jail.*

Ambrosia's world and Assata's world cross over.

AMBROSIA *preps for a bus journey, putting on her coat, etc.*

Scene 12

Ambrosia's world. The streets of Ferguson. The sound of a bus pulling up.

AMBROSIA. Does this bus go to the Ferguson municipal court? It's running late? Will it get there by nine? Great. I'll run if I have to.

AMBROSIA *stands, sits, stands again, waits impatiently.*

I can't tell my dad about these tickets; he'll take that as I broke our arrangement. 'A deal is a deal,' he'll say, then it'll be back to Pittsburgh and off to dentistry school. I am the master of my fate; I am the captain of my soul. Dad said that so much growing up, his voice rents a permanent space in my brain. I can take care of these tickets. Step one: Explain to the judge I couldn't possibly have done so much wrong in the five minutes I was talking to that officer. And how could I owe $432 in tickets? Step two: Maybe I'll cry a little. And if that doesn't work – Step three: Use my scholarship money and get beach body ready by only eating ramen noodles till my sophomore year. I can do this.

She sings bravado out the window.

I Am The Master Of My Fate, I Am The Captain Of My Soul!

(*To a bus passenger.*) Oh, excuse me.

Beat.

I can see the Ferguson jail up ahead, the place Trey has been sitting for the past two weeks. I can see his broken face…

We hear the sound of chains clinking or claps.

ASSATA *hums 'Roll Jordan Roll', a Spiritual.*

The chains/claps continue underscoring AMBROSIA *and* ASSATA.

ASSATA (*singing*). Went down to the river Jordan
 Where John baptized three
 When I walked with the devil in hell
 Said 'John ain't baptized me'.

 8:48 and I am seven minutes away – bam! Straight down that road, then one more block to go. Come on, come on, slowest. Lincoln. On. The. Planet.

She waits, signal-waves for the car to pass.

 Go ahead, I'm not late or anything!

ASSATA (*singing*). I say roll, Jordan, roll
 Roll, Jordan, roll
 My soul oughta rise in heaven, lord
 For the year when Jordan rolls.

AMBROSIA. Two minutes. Just two minutes to go, excuse me officer.

 (*To audience.*) And there leaning on the trunk of his car, just moments away from the courthouse a smiling cop stops me.

ASSATA (*singing*). I said roll, Jordan, roll.

AMBROSIA. He says: (*As police officer.*) 'You know you committed a crime back there?'

 (*As* AMBROSIA.) What crime?

 (*As police officer.*) 'Jaywalking.'

ASSATA (*singing*). Roll, Jordan, roll.

AMBROSIA (*as police officer*). 'I'm gon' have to give you a ticket for that.'

The music stops.

 'No, no, no, please I'm already late, and I can barely afford the tickets I have now.' He takes my ID –

The music returns, rising slowly.

 – slowly walks back to the front of his car. When he hands me the new ticket, he says: 'Good luck getting to court on time.' I run to the courthouse.

ASSATA *(singing).* I said roll, Jordan, roll
   Roll, Jordan, roll
   My soul oughta rise in heaven, lord
   For the year when Jordan rolls

The sound of the gavel coming down. The music stops.

AMBROSIA. 9:06.
   Six minutes late. That's not too bad.
   I once waited an hour and a half for Beyoncé to come on stage. Six minutes is fashionably late.
   The courthouse door is locked. I can hear people inside.

The sound of a banging gavel.

Dammit.

The sound of municipal court phoneline ringing.

Hi, court clerk, please. Hi. I have a court date today and I'm here but the door is locked and I can't get in – Ambrosia Rollins, August 9, 1995. Well how much is the 'failure to appear' charge? $125! The tickets are already $432… How am I suppose to pay all this – I'm sorry can you repeat that? So, that's $125 for 'failure to appear and a $50 fee for the judge to issue a warrant, plus 56 cents for every mile the cops have to drive to serve me the warrant—wait! You mean a warrant warrant? Like they'll arrest me? Isn't that what happens when a cop serves a warrant?!

She listens, getting more agitated.

I can't pay you right now, I don't get my scholarship check till the third, but it's not enough to pay it all. I can pay you $80, can I do that? Please let me do that! I'M AT THE COURTHOUSE THEY WON'T LET ME IN!!! I can't go to jail, I didn't do anything to go – hello? hello?!

(*Looking at the phone, stunned.*) I am the master of my fate, I am the captain of my soul.

The sound of a banging gavel.

Lights fade out on AMBROSIA.

Scene 12.5

Assata's world. At the courthouse. ASSATA *stands in a pool of light.*

ASSATA. You jury members should know –

EVELYN. Joanne –

ASSATA. – this crooked judge is appointed by Nixon.

EVELYN. I can handle this –

ASSATA. Kamau and I are being persecuted for our political beliefs.

EVELYN. Your honor, I strongly object to the FBI's request, to photograph my client in the same wig, clothes and glasses as the woman pictured robbing the bank –

ASSATA. I'm not gonna help you build evidence to justify your lies.

EVELYN *crosses to hand the wig, glasses and dress to* ASSATA.

EVELYN. Let the record reflect that we object to the judge's orders to have my client photographed by using force.

ASSATA *begins to shuffle, refusing to take the photo. As she speaks, she continues to try to say the statements below but never manages to say it all the way through.*
'*In the spirit of those unjustly and illegally charged before me.*'

ASSATA (*protesting*). In the –

EVELYN. Let the record reflect the marshals are shoving my client.

ASSATA. In the spir–

EVELYN. Let the record reflect that the marshals are twisting my client's arm.

ASSATA. Unjustly –

EVELYN. Let the record reflect that five marshals are manhandling my client –

ASSATA. In the spirit –

EVELYN. Let the record reflect that the marshals are twisting both my clients arms –

ASSATA. In the –

EVELYN. Let the record reflect five marshals are kicking my client.

ASSATA. Stop it!

EVELYN. Let the record reflect they are jerking my client.

ASSATA. Illegally –

EVELYN. They are punching my client.

ASSATA. In the –

EVELYN. Kicking my client.

ASSATA. Is that too much to ask for?

EVELYN. In –

Let the record reflect –

ASSATA. Unjustly –

EVELYN. Let the record reflect –

ASSATA stops speaking, as she's restrained.

Let the record reflect, five marshals are restraining my client while photos are being taken.

ASSATA lies on the floor, listless. We hear the sound of camera shuttering.

An image appears on the screen with ASSATA's photo superimposed over the black-and-white photo of the bank robbery.

We hear the sound of camera shutters.

Scene 13

AMBROSIA *and* ASSATA *both move into isolation.*
AMBROSIA *is at friend's house hiding.* ASSATA, *in a prison cell. 'Wanna Be Free' plays.*

AMBROSIA (*singing*). My heart is rushing fast
  My blood is turning black
  My feet can't move fast enough

ASSATA (*singing*). Gotta clear my name
  Gotta find a way
  To get back where I was before

AMBROSIA (*singing*). Making a little bit of cash
  My money's going away fast
  Trying to keep up with all these bills
  Mama's calling from the past
  A time when smiles never masked the pain that's new for me now.

ASSATA and AMBROSIA (*singing*). And I know
  I just wanna be free
  Oh, I just wanna be free
  And I know
  I just wanna be free
  I wanna be free.

AMBROSIA. Assata said:

ASSATA *and* AMBROSIA. Nobody in the world, nobody in history, has ever gotten their freedom by appealing to the moral sense of the people who were oppressing them.

So, I ran. I ran to my friend Tanya's and I haven't left in three weeks.

ASSATA. I've been on trial for weeks. Hauled from jail to courthouse
  Courthouse to jail, thrown in solitary confinement.
  Which ain't living, barely existing.

AMBROSIA. Mom and Dad have been calling me every day since I went into hiding. What am I supposed to say?

Sorry Mom, sorry Dad, I haven't been to school in three weeks 'cause there's a warrant out for my arrest. They wouldn't listen, or even understand, how I'm officially a fugitive.

ASSATA and AMBROSIA (*singing*). And I know
I just wanna be free
Oh,
I just wanna be free and I know
I just wanna be free
Oh, I just wanna be free.

This vamp continues with adlibs and harmonies to the end of the song.

ASSATA. Me and my alleged co-conspirator, Kamau, refused to be railroaded by this miscarriage of justice. We'd protest everyday telling the jury what a sham trial this is. The judge got angry, and completely banned us from court.

But as Kamau and I sat in that little room, listening to the trial drag on and on, we found hope in each other. 'Cause for the first time in years, we had privacy and time to reconnect – to remember what it feels like to be alive. To love.

And from that love came our beautiful daughter, Kakuya, who was born in prison.

AMBROSIA. Trey came to see me at Tanya's. He'd sat in jail for two weeks waiting to see a judge. The judge wasn't interested in hearing his arguments about arresting someone without probable cause was a violation of their Fourth Amendment rights. He just wanted Trey to pay the fine and move along, $2400!! Trey's got a trial date, but it's not till next year. So he waited a week before he got a hold of his cousin to pay a bail bondsman. But they just took his money and transferred him to the jail in Florissant 'cause he had a warrant for 'rolling through a stop sign'. The Black Student Union paid his tickets there, but they just took his money and transferred him over to the jail in Jennings 'cause he had a warrant for 'failure to comply'. People around here call that the money-shuffle. Trey was only able to get out because his student-loan check came in, and he used that money to set himself free.

ASSATA. My mother brings my daughter, Kakuya, out to visit me every week. Kakuya calls me Mama Assata and she calls my mother, Mama. It's been four years of the pitiful visits, four years of missed birthdays, and countless broken promises that I'd be coming home soon. But I'm praying that after this trial – this last hurdle – I'll go home.

ASSATA. When I see

AMBROSIA. When I see

ASSATA. My daughter.

AMBROSIA. Trey.

ASSATA. I can't help but touch her face.

AMBROSIA. I can't help but touch his face.

AMBROSIA. Run my finger down the pale skin of his scar where the police beat him.

ASSATA. She looks different today. A pain and sorrow in her face I've never seen before.

AMBROSIA. Trey told me he thought they'd whacked his eyeball out 'cause he couldn't see a thing out of it. Total blackness. But when the nurse washed the blood away, and the swelling went down as he sat in jail. He could see he wasn't blind. Just now that eye's always gonna droop lower than the other. He moves my hand away and jokes, 'They say men with scars are sexy.'

ASSATA. I do all I can to connect with my baby.

(*Singing*.) The wheels on the bus
Go round and round
Round and round
Round and round –

AMBROSIA. When I was in elementary school there was this girl who would always pass out when she saw blood.

Momma explained that when that little girl would see blood. She'd internalize that bleeding as her own… That's empathy. That's humanity.

But to beat a person with a baton and watch him bleed.

To be able to desecrate another body, lock him away, take away his freedom. It's a dangerous blindness when you can't see another person as human.

ASSATA. 'Kakuya, Mommy loves you,' I say.

'You're not my mother!' She screams. 'You can get outta here. You could leave if you wanted to!'

I try to hug her, but she starts punching me, pulling away. She runs to the prison doors, and starts kicking them, hitting them, and throwing all the energy from her little body until she's spent.

Then she turns to look at me, a helplessness on her face I can't… I sorry, baby. I'm so so sorry.

AMBROSIA. I shudder. And it breaks the silence of me and Trey's bodies. I want to protect Trey. So I pull his face to mine and kiss him, feeling like I can kiss away the scar on his skin, the scar on his soul.

ASSATA. I grab Kakuya and I hold her so tight: 'I'm sorry, baby. I'm so so sorry.' She lies in my arms. So still.

AMBROSIA. And I know I wanna be free
I wanna be free
I wanna be free

ASSATA. And I know I wanna be free
I wanna be free
I wanna be free

Scene 14

Assata's world. The courthouse, 1978. The sound of a court gavel banging.

ASSATA. I keep going over that night.
  What if we didn't go out?
  Or stop for gas.
  Checked the brake lights.
  Taken a different route.
  We knew the cops on the Jersey Turnpike were out for blood.
  What if I just... stayed. I'd still be free.

May 2, 1973.

I'm on the New Jersey Turnpike with Zayd and Sundiata. Red and blue lights start flashing behind us. Shit, Zayd. I told you the tail light was dim. They're gonna know me. My face is everywhere. There's no way out of it this time. What if I just stayed silent, this time. Yes sir, Mister Trooper sir. Maybe because I'm a woman –

ASSATA *kneels. Her hands still in the air.*

they might take me in nice and easy.

It's late.
I won't talk back 'cause I don't know what they might do.

The sound of gunshots.

ASSATA *sings the chorus of 'Oh Freedom', a Spiritual.*

Mouth dirty.
Grit.
Arm numb.
Body aching.

I hear them asking, 'Is she dead yet? Is she dead yet?'

A video of water plays, pictures of Cuba. The sound of ASSATA *talking to her* GRANDMOTHER.

AMBROSIA. Assata sat in jail for six years.
  Enduring brutality after brutality.

Going from trial to trial.
Armed robbery. Dismissed.
Bank robbery. Acquitted.
Kidnap of a drug dealer. Acquitted.
Murder of a drug dealer. Acquitted.
Attempted murder of a police officer. Dismissed.
Finally, murder of a state trooper on the New Jersey Turnpike May 2nd 1973. Convicted.

GRANDMOTHER (*voice-over*). Assata, did you hear me?

ASSATA (*voice-over*). Yeah, Grandma, I can hear you.

Meanwhile, ASSATA *rises, she opens a suitcase and takes out her clothes to change into.*

GRANDMA (*voice-over*). Did you hear what I said? You're getting out!

ASSATA (*voice-over*). What?

GRANDMOTHER (*voice-over*). I saw it, in my dream. You're getting out! We were in our old house in Jamaica, you remember that old house? We were there. And I was dressing you. I saw it just as clear as the nose on your face.

AMBROSIA *helps* ASSATA *clean and slowly get changed.*

Together, they hop onto a 'boat' and begin to row away as the voiceover plays.

ASSATA (*voice-over*). You were dressing me?!

GRANDMOTHER (*voice-over*). I know what you're thinking. But you were alive, and as you are now. I saw it plain as day, baby. You getting out.

Don't get too comfortable, you gon' be free.

ASSATA *and* AMBROSIA *reach their destination.*

AMBROSIA *performs a type of cleansing ritual on* ASSATA*, and bids* ASSATA *adieu.*

ASSATA *walks in a circle basking in the warmth and newfound freedom she's achieved.*

'Oh Freedom' begins to play.

ASSATA (*voice-over*). Every time a Black Freedom Fighter is
murdered or captured, the pigs try to create the impression
that they have quashed the movement, destroyed our forces,
and put down the Black Revolution. The pigs also try to
give the impression that five or ten guerrillas are responsible
for every revolutionary action carried out in Amerika. That
is nonsense. That is absurd. Black revolutionaries don't
just drop from the moon. We are created by our conditions.
Shaped by our oppression. We have declared war on the rich
who prosper on our poverty, the politicians who lie to us
with smiling faces, and all the mindless, heartless robots who
protect them and their property. They paint us as vicious,
brutal, mad-dog criminals. It should be clear, it must be clear
to anyone who can think, see or hear that we are the victims.
The victims and not the criminals. And until every Black
man, woman, and child is free, there will always be a Black
Liberation Army.

The music continues.

Scene 15

Ambrosia's world. In her dorm room, AMBROSIA *sits still holding Assata's biography.*

AMBROSIA. Assata, in fear of her life, broke out of prison in
1979 and fled to Cuba. Where she continues to live in exile
to this day. Never can return home again. Assata said, 'If you
are deaf, dumb, and blind to what's happening in the world,
you're under no obligation to do anything. But if you know
what's happening and do nothing but sit on your ass, then
you're nothing but a punk.'

(*Singing*.) They say freedom only comes
To those who do something to move it.
They say freedom only comes
To those who do something to grow it.

Arm yourself with courage and strength
Tell yourself that you can win
And push naysayers aside,
Take a deep breath,
You're gonna be fine
And point your head straight up to the sky. Keep saying
I gotta get out of here
No time to look back no time for fear.
Keep saying
I gotta get out of here
No time to look back no time for fear.
I gotta stop hiding
There's no way,
That my problems will disappear someday
I gotta start fighting
There's a way
Just listen to my heart
I'll find the right words to say arm yourself with courage and strength
Tell yourself that you can win just push naysayers aside,
Tell yourself that you'll be fine
And point your head straight up to the sky. Keep saying
I gotta get out of here
No time to look back no time for fear.
Keep saying
I gotta get out of here
No time to look back no time for fear.

I made the decision to come out of hiding. I took out a student loan to pay for my tickets. I got a job to pay back the student loan. And I went back to my life. But it's not the same. 'Cause it's like, I've been walking around in the dark and I was finally seeing the light. And I don't know how I feel about it. On August 9, 2014, just before I got to college, Officer Darren Wilson of the Ferguson police force shot and killed an unarmed teenager as he was walking through his neighborhood. Today, November 24, 2014, after a three-month trial, the jury are prepared to give their verdict. The air in St. Louis is cold and restless. Trey and I go down to the courthouse at sunset to hear the verdict. There are hundreds of people here: Black, White, Latino. All the same. All want justice for Mike Brown. Trey says, no matter what happens we stay together. I see militarized police. The tanks. They're preparing for war, so should we? It's after dark: 8:15 p.m. We're all pressed in together. I can't hear the radio broadcasting the news but someone says they're announcing the verdict. I see Mike Brown's mother up on a platform; she covers her face and sobs.

The sound of a drone is heard.

A murmur of disgust ripples through the group. The man who murdered her son will walk free.

We hear ASSATA *humming 'Ain't Gonna Let Nobody', a Spiritual, but the melody is free – not in time.*

We all stand stunned, disbelieving for maybe a whole minute. Then the revelation begins to whip over the crowd like hurricane winds across the ocean. Churning and roiling, everyone begins to move at once, 'This is not justice! This is not justice!' Anger shakes down the metal police barricade, pushing it to the ground. 'Get out of here, you pigs!' The police, dressed black in riot gear and helmets, armed with batons, move into position ready to wage war with us dressed in winter coats and scarves, armed with anger. I hold tight to Trey's hand, we move against the rushing tide of people, away from the courthouse. As we're moving, I hear singing:

ASSATA *appears, ethereal.*

Her voice almost echoing AMBROSIA*'s, not overpowering.*

ASSATA (*singing*). Ain't gonna let nobody turn me around
　Turn me around,
　Turn me around
　Ain't gonna let nobody turn me around
　I'm gonna keep on walking,
　Keep on talking,
　Walking up the freedom land.

AMBROSIA. People start throwing rocks and water bottles against the police shields.

They sing.

ASSATA *and* AMBROSIA (*singing*). Ain't gonna let nobody
Turn me around,
Turn me around,
Turn me around.

AMBROSIA. There's breaking glass and the hiss of a hot fire. People are chanting: 'They say move back, we say fight back. Move back, Fight back! Move back, Fight back! Black Lives Matter! Black Lives Matter! Black Lives Matter!'

ASSATA *begins humming 'Ain't Gonna Let Nobody' again.*

I hear a soft boom, boom, boom then the sound of metal canisters skidding across the asphalt. A white smoke drifts in the air and punches me in the lungs.

(*She gasps, coughing.*) 'It's tear gas,' Trey tells me. 'Hold your breath! Close your eyes.' My face is wet with snot and tears. The pain is so… violent. A voice over the speaker says, 'This is no longer a peaceful protest. Please evacuate the area.'

(*To* TREY.) Can you see? I can't see! 'Hold still,' Trey tells me. I feel liquid falling over my eyes and mouth, the pain still clings to my face. It feels like forever before I can see again. I hear, someone being beaten; baton hitting bone. A police car, overturned. Burned. And singing, in the midst of all this chaos.

ASSATA *moves forward, still softly singing.*

I squint. I see people holding Mike Brown's mother; giving their strength to her. She is no longer crying. And there's something about that image that gives me… hope. We have survived war and plague, disaster and pain, and even slavery by holding on to each other. By never ever giving up.

AMBROSIA *looks to* ASSATA, *a new realization overcoming her.*

Revolutionaries are formed through the mud.

AMBROSIA *extends her arm to* ASSATA *who joins her.*

And it is our duty to fight for our freedom. It is our duty to win.

ASSATA *and* AMBROSIA. We must love each other and support each other; we have nothing to lose but our chains.

AMBROSIA *listens to the protestors around her and feels herself coming into her new self.*

She has become a fearless fighter and knows what she must do.

They say move back. We say fight back. Move back. Fight back. Move back. Fight back. Black Lives Matter! Black Lives Matter! Black Lives Matter! Black Lives Matter!

AMBROSIA *sings.*

ASSATA *stomps in time.*

The sound of marching.

Ain't gonna let nobody turn me around,
Turn me around,
Turn me around
Ain't gonna let nobody turn me around,
I'm gonna keep on walking,
Keep on talking
Walking up to freedom land.

They sing.

ASSATA *and* AMBROSIA. Ain't gonna let no policeman turn me around,
Turn me around, turn me around
Ain't let no policeman turn me around,
I'm gonna keep on walking, keep on talking,
Marching up to freedom land.

Ain't gonna let no jailhouse turn me around
Turn me around, turn me around,

Ain't gonna let no jailhouse turn me around,
I'm gonna keep on walking, keep on talking
Marching up to freedom land.

Ain't gonna let no policeman turn me around,
Turn me around, turn me around,
Ain't let no policeman turn me around,
I'm gonna keep on walking, keep on talking,
Marching up to freedom land.

Ain't gonna let no jailhouse turn me around,
Turn me around, turn me around,
Ain't gonna let no jailhouse turn me around,
I'm gonna keep on walking, keep on talking
Marching up to freedom land.

A loud boom is heard.

Blackout.

End.

A Nick Hern Book

Through the Mud first published in Great Britain as a paperback original in 2024 by Nick Hern Books Limited, The Glasshouse, 49a Goldhawk Road, London, W12 8QP, in association with Steller Quines and The Royal Lyceum Theatre Edinburgh

Through the Mud copyright © 2024 Apphia Campbell

Apphia Campbell has asserted her right to be identified as the author of this work

Cover design by Steph Pyne

Designed and typeset by Nick Hern Books, London
Printed in Great Britain by Mimeo Ltd, Huntingdon, Cambridgeshire PE29 6XX

A CIP catalogue record for this book is available from the British Library

ISBN 978 1 83904 387 1

CAUTION All rights whatsoever in this play are strictly reserved. Requests to reproduce the text in whole or in part should be addressed to the publisher.

Amateur Performing Rights Applications for performance, including readings and excerpts, by amateurs in the English language should be addressed to the Performing Rights Manager, Nick Hern Books, The Glasshouse, 49a Goldhawk Road, London W12 8QP, *tel* +44 (0)20 8749 4953, *email* rights@nickhernbooks.co.uk, except as follows:

Australia: ORiGiN Theatrical, *tel* +61 (2) 8514 5201, *email* enquiries@originmusic.com.au, *web* www.origintheatrical.com.au

New Zealand: Play Bureau, 20 Rua Street, Mangapapa, Gisborne 4010, *tel* +64 21 258 3998, *email* info@playbureau.com

Professional Performing Rights Rights Applications for performance by professionals in any medium and in any language throughout the world should be addressed in the first instance to Nick Hern Books, see contact details above.

No performance of any kind may be given unless a licence has been obtained. Applications should be made before rehearsals begin. Publication of this play does not necessarily indicate its availability for amateur performance.

www.nickhernbooks.co.uk/environmental-policy

www.nickhernbooks.co.uk

facebook.com/nickhernbooks

twitter.com/nickhernbooks